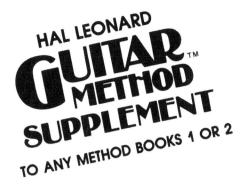

HAL LEONARD
Guitar Method SUPPLEMENT
TO ANY METHOD BOOKS 1 OR 2

Chris for 1, 2, or 3 Guitars

by Will Schmid

Contents

HAL•LEONARD®
CORPORATION

7777 W. BLUEMOUND RD. P.O. BOX 13819 MILWAUKEE, WI 53213

About the Author

Will Schmid is the author of the internationally acclaimed **Hal Leonard Guitar Method System** (available in 8 languages). He received his BA from Luther College and his PhD from the Eastman School of Music. Dr. Schmid has authored over 40 books, cassettes and a videotape for guitar, banjo, wind and string instruments. He has given workshops throughout the United States and in Canada, Australia and Europe. He is a Past President of the Wisconsin Music Educators Conference. He is currently Professor of Music at the University of Wisconsin-Milwaukee and serves on the editorial staff of the Hal Leonard Publishing Corporation.

Will Schmid

Dedication

This collection of Christmas songs is dedicated to all of the wonderful teachers, choir and instrumental directors and adult leaders who every year give children the opportunity to learn about this rich cultural heritage.

In particular I would like to thank my own church choir directors, Dagne Hinton and Geraldine Ritzenthaler, and my high school director, James Coates, who gave me so much support and encouragement in Springfield, Minnesota when I was a boy. These opportunities to sing and play in a wide variety of contexts have helped me immeasureably throughout my music career.

How to Use This Book

This book is playable by 1, 2, or 3 guitars (or guitar ensemble/class). Each arrangement features the melody (lead), a harmony (2nd) part and a rhythm part (the chords) as follows:

Strums and Finger Picks are indicated by number in a box at the upper left-hand corner of each arrangement. The numbers correspond to the strums (1-6) and finger picks (7-12) found on the chart on page 30 of this book. For more help with accompaniment patterns you may wish to refer to the Hal Leonard's *Strums for Guitar* or *Fingerpicks for Guitar*.

1 guitar	•Play the Melody (Lead) •Record one or two of the parts and play the remaining part. This can be done with the simplest cassette recorder or in a more sophisticated way with the new multi-track recorders. You may wish to add bass or percussion if you have 4-track equipment.

2 guitars	•Play the Melody and the Harmony parts. •Play the Melody and the Rhythm parts. •Record one of the parts and play the other two along with the recording. You may wish to add a bass part playing from the chord symbols.

3 guitars	•Play all three parts together; then switch parts and play again.

Chords - Look up any chords that you don't know on the chord chart on page 31.

Angels We Have Heard On High

4, 6, 11, 12

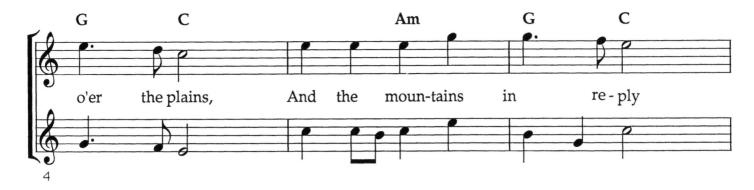

An - gels we have heard on high Sweet-ly sing - ing

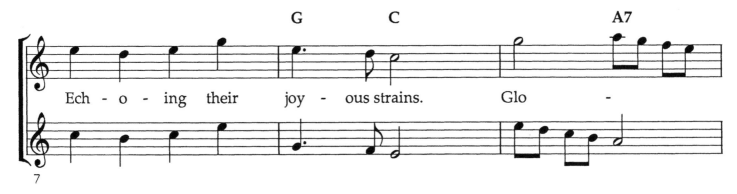

o'er the plains, And the moun-tains in re - ply

Ech - o - ing their joy - ous strains. Glo -

- - - - - ri - a

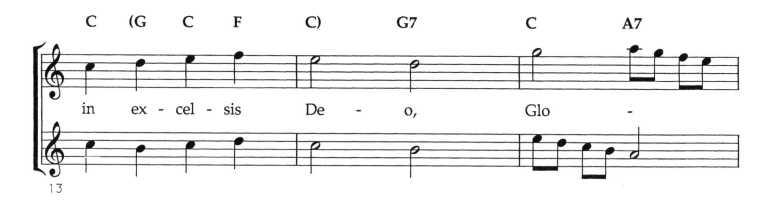

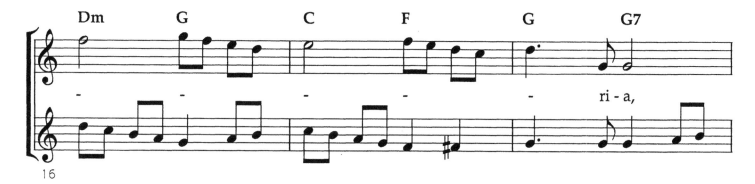

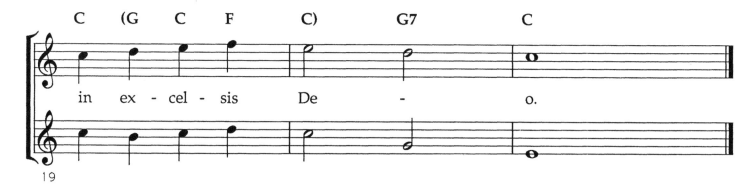

Away in a Manger (I)

1, 2, 3, 7, 8, 9

A - way in a__ man-ger no crib for a bed. The

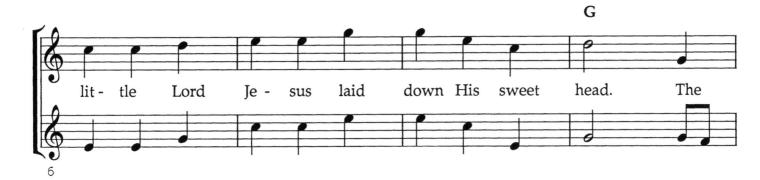

lit - tle Lord Je - sus laid down His sweet head. The

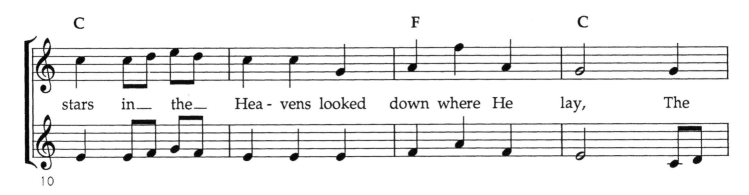

stars in__ the__ Hea - vens looked down where He lay, The

lit - tle Lord Je - sus a - sleep on the hay.

Away in a Manger (II)

1, 2, 3, 7, 8, 9

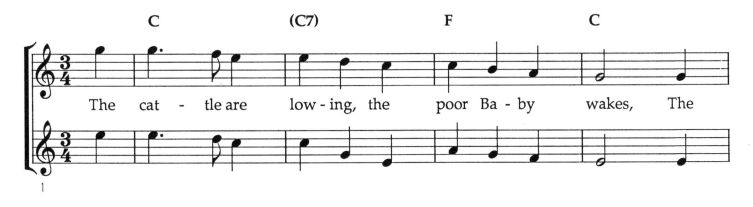

The cat - tle are low - ing, the poor Ba - by wakes, The

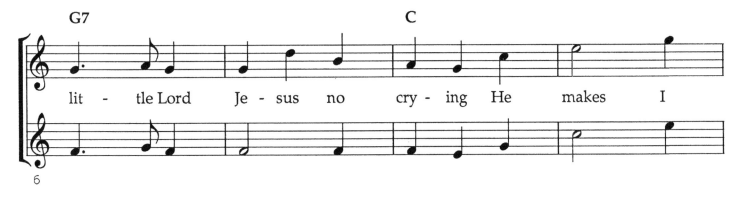

lit - tle Lord Je - sus no cry - ing He makes I

love Thee, Lord Je - sus! Look down from the sky, And

stay by my cra - dle, Till morn - ing is nigh.

Bring a Torch, Jeannette, Isabella

1, 3, 7, 9

Bring a torch, Jean - nette, Is - a - bel - la, Bring a

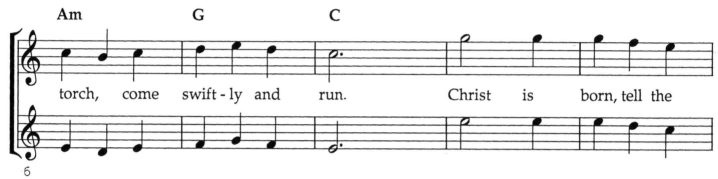

torch, come swift - ly and run. Christ is born, tell the

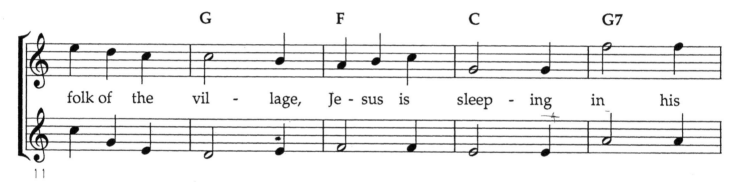

folk of the vil - lage, Je - sus is sleep - ing in his

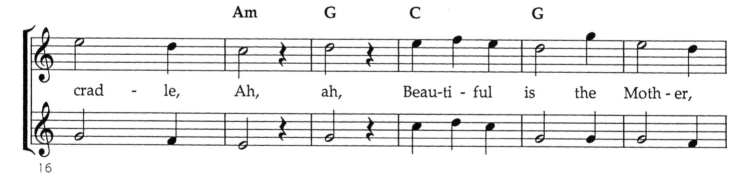

crad - le, Ah, ah, Beau - ti - ful is the Moth - er,

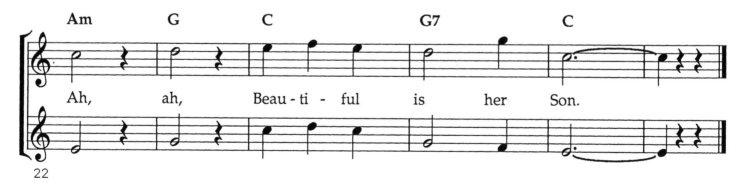

Ah, ah, Beau - ti - ful is her Son.

8

Deck the Hall

4, 5, 6, 10, 11, 12

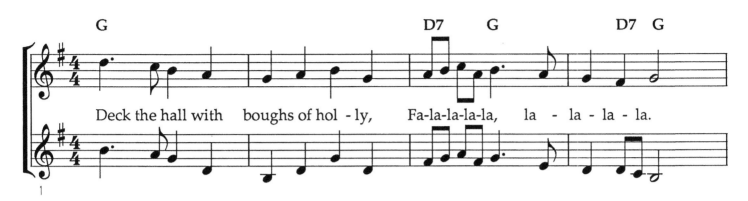

Deck the hall with boughs of hol - ly, Fa-la-la-la-la, la - la - la - la.

'Tis the sea -son to be jol - ly, Fa-la-la-la-la, la - la - la - la.

Don we now our gay ap-par - rel, Fa-la-la - la-la-la, la - la - la.

Troll the an - cient Yule-tide car - ol, Fa-la-la-la-la, la - la - la - la.

Go Tell It on the Mountain

4, 5, 6, 10, 11, 12

Go, tell it on the moun - tain, Ov-er the hills and

ev - ery where, Go, tell it on the moun - tain, that

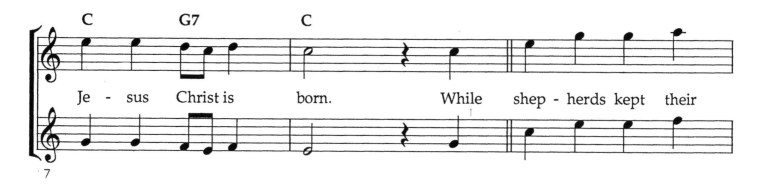

Je - sus Christ is born. While shep - herds kept their

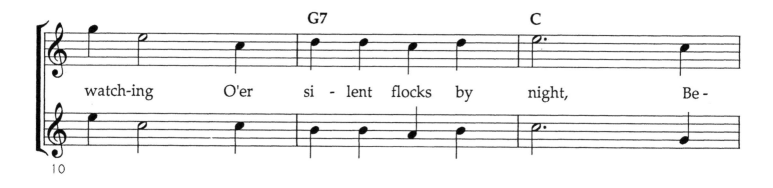

watch-ing O'er si - lent flocks by night, Be -

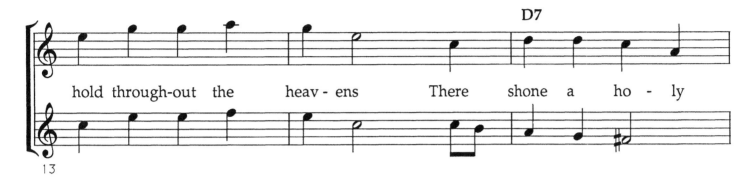

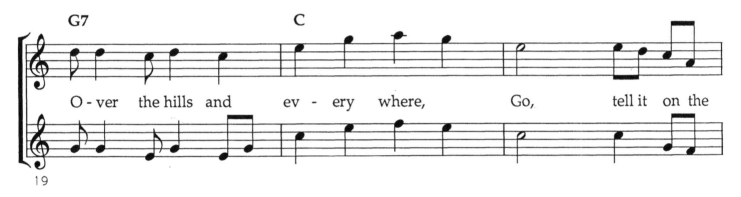

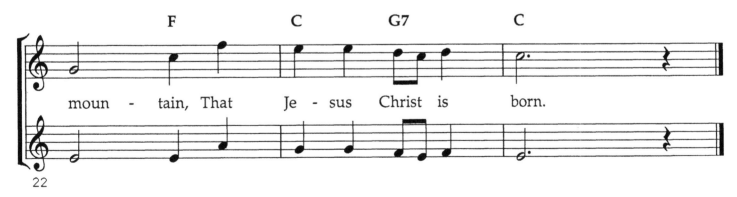

God Rest Ye Merry, Gentlemen

4, 10, 11, 12

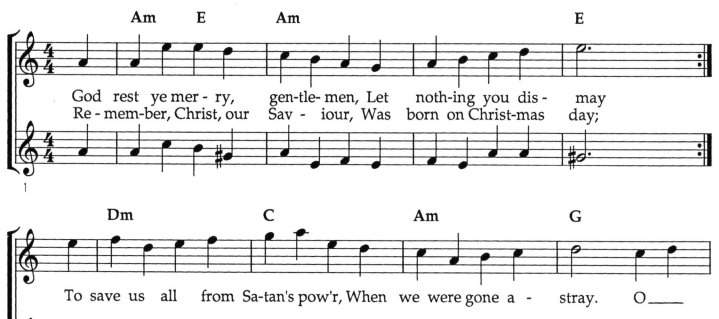

God rest ye mer - ry, gen-tle- men, Let noth-ing you dis - may
Re - mem-ber, Christ, our Sav - iour, Was born on Christ-mas day;

To save us all from Sa-tan's pow'r, When we were gone a - stray. O____

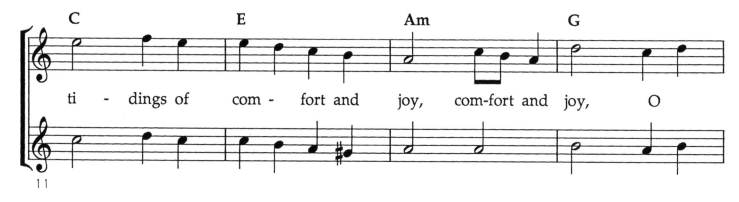

ti - dings of com - fort and joy, com-fort and joy, O

ti - dings of com - fort and joy._____

Good King Wenceslas

4, 6, 10, 11, 12

The Holly and the Ivy

1, 2, 3, 7, 8, 9

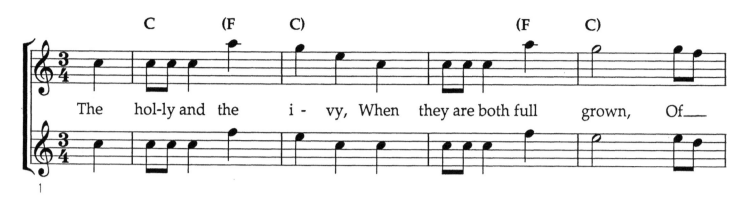

The hol-ly and the i - vy, When they are both full grown, Of

all the trees that are in the wood, The hol-ly bears the crown; The

ris-ing of the sun, And the run-ning of the deer; The

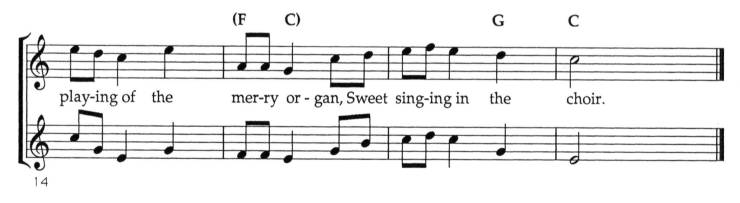

play-ing of the mer-ry or - gan, Sweet sing-ing in the choir.

Jolly Old Saint Nicholas

4, 10, 11, 12

Jol - ly Old Saint Nich - o - las   Lean your ear this   way!

Don't you tell a   sin - gle   soul   what I'm going to   say;

Christ-mas Eve is   com-ing soon,   Now, you dear old   man,

Whis-per what you'll bring to   me,   Tell me if   you   can.

Jingle Bells

4, 10, 11, 12

Dash-ing through the snow in a one-horse o - pen sleigh.

O'er the fields we go Laugh-ing all the way.

Bells on bob- tail ring, mak-ing spir - its bright. What

fun it is to ride and sing a sleigh- ing song to - night. Oh,

Joy to the World

4, 11, 12

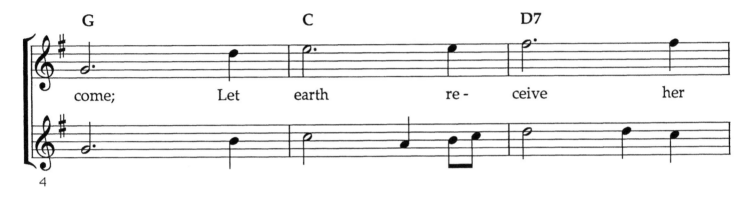

sing.   And— heav'n and na - ture— sing,   And—

heav'n   and   heav'n_____ and   na - ture   sing.

O Come, Little Children

4, 5, 6, 10, 11, 12

O come, lit - tle chil - dren, o come, one and all, To

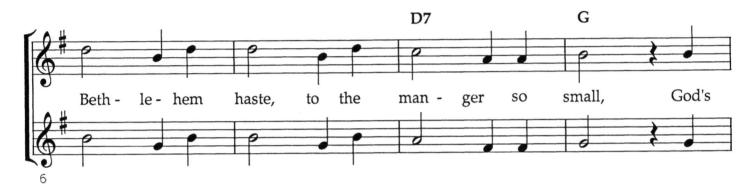

Beth - le - hem haste, to the man - ger so small, God's

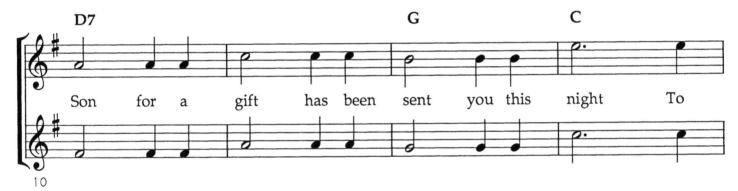

Son for a gift has been sent you this night To

be your re - deem - er, your joy and de - light.

Patapan

4, 5, 6, 10, 11, 12

Wil-lie take your lit - tle drum, With your whis - tle Rob - in

come! When we hear the fife and drum, Tu-re-lu-re-

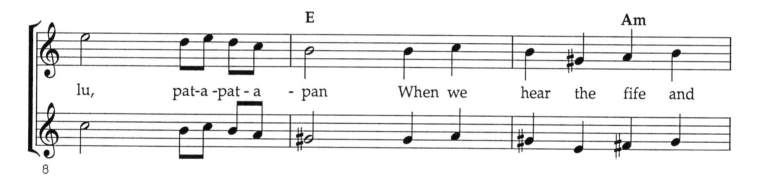

lu, pat-a -pat - a - pan When we hear the fife and

drum, Christ-mas should be fro - lic - some.

Silent Night

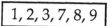

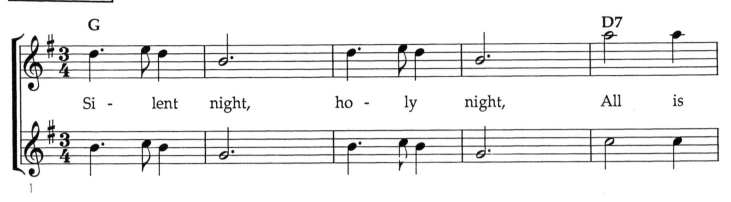

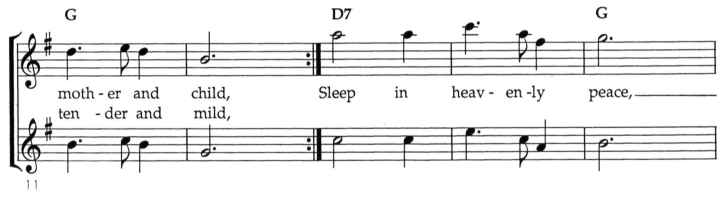

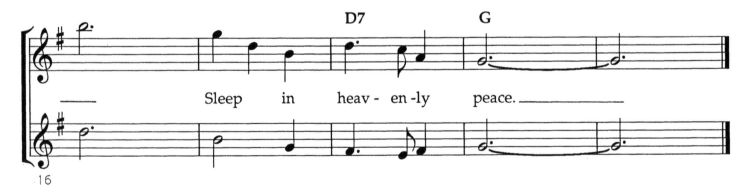

We Wish You a Merry Christmas

1, 3, 7, 8, 9

We wish you a mer-ry Christ-mas, We wish you a mer-ry Christ-mas, We

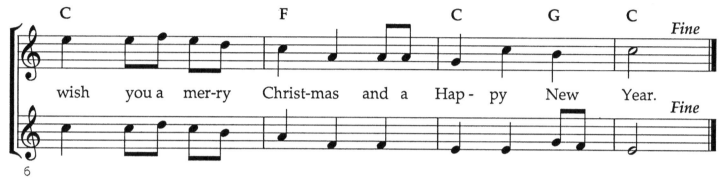

wish you a mer-ry Christ-mas and a Hap - py New Year.

Fine

Good tid - ings we bring to you and your friends, Good

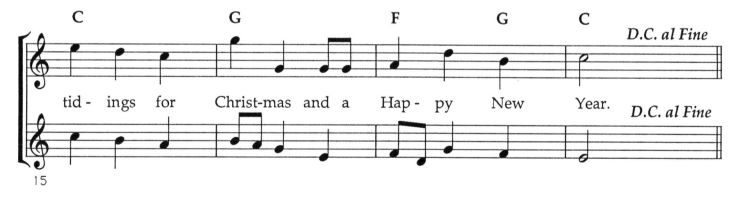

tid - ings for Christ-mas and a Hap - py New Year.

D.C. al Fine

What Child is This?

1, 2, 3, 7, 8, 9

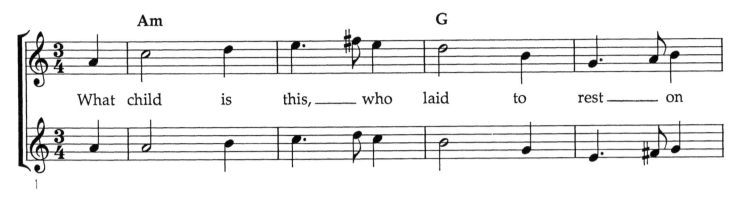

What child is this, _____ who laid to rest _____ on

Ma - ry's lap is sleep - ing? Whom

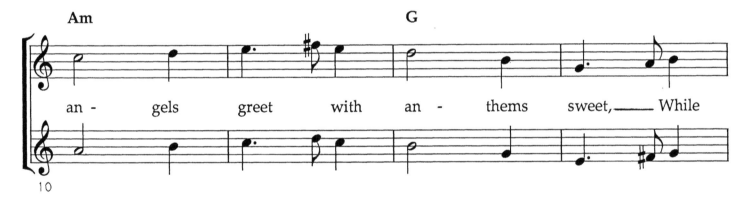

an - gels greet with an - thems sweet, _____ While

shep - herds watch _____ are keep - ing.

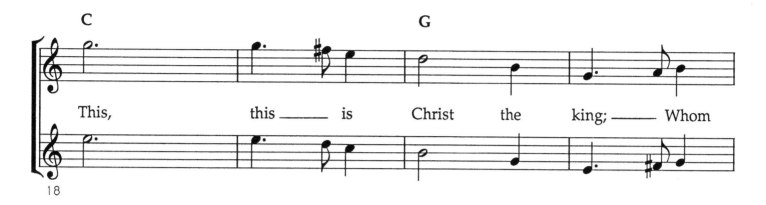

This,   this ____ is   Christ   the   king; ____ Whom

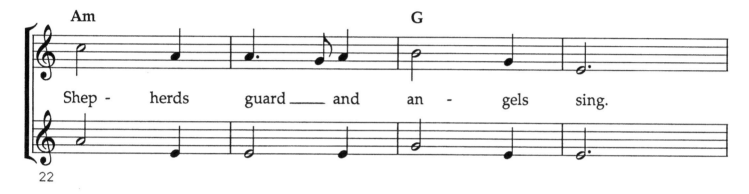

Shep - herds   guard ____ and   an - gels   sing.

Haste,   — haste ____ to   bring   Him   laud, ____ The

Babe, ____ the   Son ____ of   Ma - ry!

Still, Still, Still

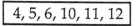

The Friendly Beasts

1, 2, 3, 7, 8, 9

Unison and chords

1. Je-sus our broth - er, strong and good, was hum - bly born in a sta - ble rude. The friend - ly beasts a - round him stood. Je - sus, our broth - er, strong and good.

Duet and chords

2. "I," said the don - key, shag-gy and brown, "I car-ried his moth - er up-hill and down, I car-ried her safe - ly to Beth-le-hem town." "I," said the don - key shag-gy and brown.

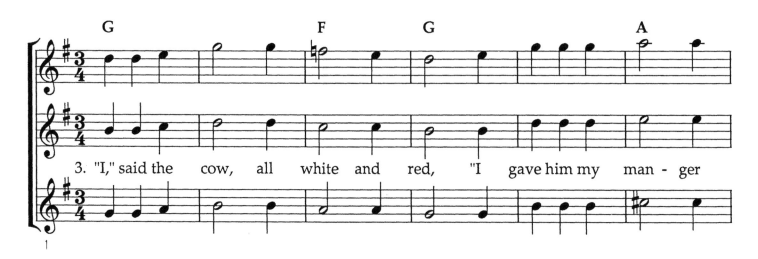

3. "I," said the cow, all white and red, "I gave him my man - ger

for his bed, I gave him my hay to pil-low his head."

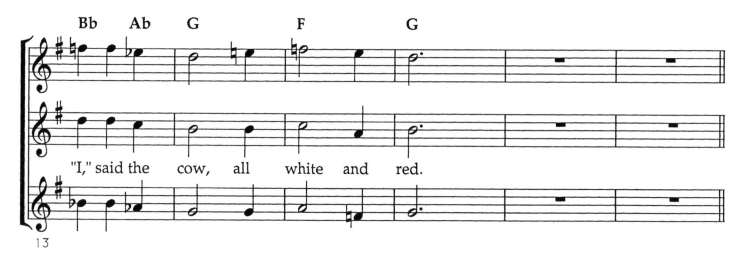

"I," said the cow, all white and red.

4. "I," said the sheep with cur - ly horn, "I gave him my wool for a blan - ket warm, He wore my coat on Christ - mas morn." "I," said the sheep with cur - ly horn.

Unison and chords

5. So ev-ery beast by some good spell, in the sta - ble dark was glad to tell of the gift he gave Im - man - u - el. The gift he gave Im - man - u - el.

Guide to Strums and Finger Picks

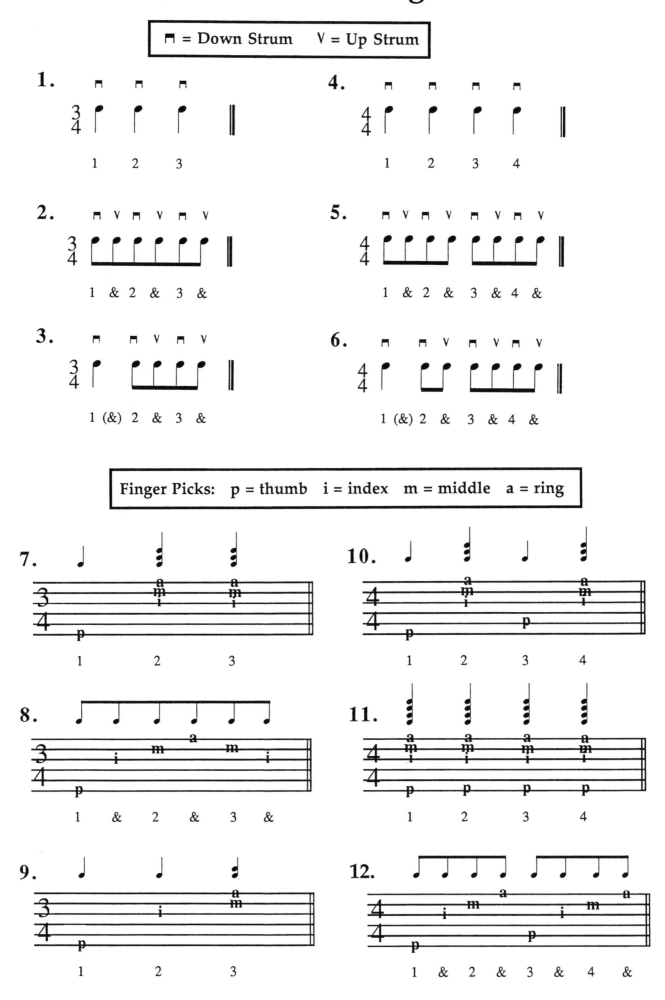

CHORD CHART

In this chart you will find all the chords you learned in this book. There are also several of the more common chords you may see in other music you are playing.

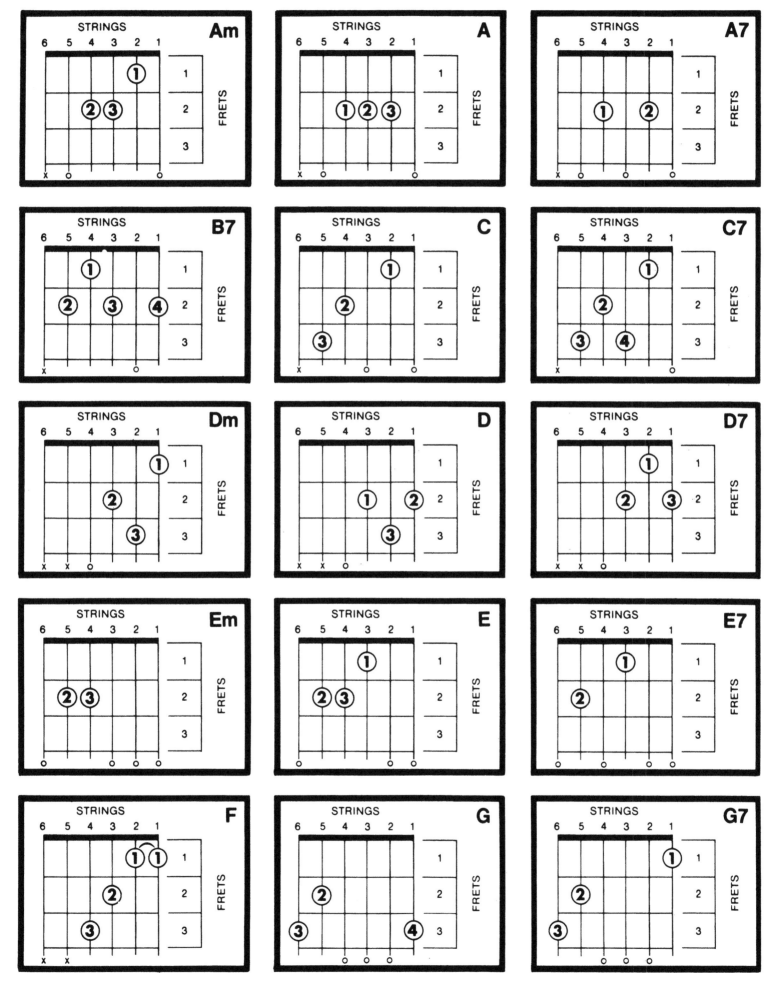

HAL LEONARD GUITAR METHOD

METHOD BOOKS, SONGBOOKS AND REFERENCE BOOKS

THE HAL LEONARD GUITAR METHOD is designed for anyone just learning to play acoustic or electric guitar. It is based on years of teaching guitar students of all ages, and it also reflects some of the best guitar teaching ideas from around the world. This comprehensive method includes: A learning sequence carefully paced with clear instructions; popular songs which increase the incentive to learn to play; versatility – can be used as self-instruction or with a teacher; audio accompaniments so that students have fun and sound great while practicing.

BOOK 1
00699010	Book Only	$9.99
00699027	Book/Online Audio	$14.99
00697341	Book/Online Audio + DVD	$27.99
00697318	DVD Only	$19.99
00155480	Deluxe Beginner Edition (Book, CD, DVD, Online Audio/ Video & Chord Poster)	$22.99

COMPLETE (BOOKS 1, 2 & 3)
00699040	Book Only	$19.99
00697342	Book/Online Audio	$27.99

BOOK 2
00699020	Book Only	$9.99
00697313	Book/Online Audio	$14.99

BOOK 3
00699030	Book Only	$9.99
00697316	Book/Online Audio	$14.99

Prices, contents and availability subject to change without notice.

STYLISTIC METHODS

ACOUSTIC GUITAR
00697347	Method Book/Online Audio	$19.99
00237969	Songbook/Online Audio	$17.99

BLUEGRASS GUITAR
00697405	Method Book/Online Audio	$19.99

BLUES GUITAR
00697326	Method Book/Online Audio (9" x 12")	$16.99
00697344	Method Book/Online Audio (6" x 9")	$15.99
00697385	Songbook/Online Audio (9" x 12")	$16.99
00248636	Kids Method Book/Online Audio	$14.99

BRAZILIAN GUITAR
00697415	Method Book/Online Audio	$17.99

CHRISTIAN GUITAR
00695947	Method Book/Online Audio	$17.99

CLASSICAL GUITAR
00697376	Method Book/Online Audio	$16.99

COUNTRY GUITAR
00697337	Method Book/Online Audio	$24.99

FINGERSTYLE GUITAR
00697378	Method Book/Online Audio	$22.99
00697432	Songbook/Online Audio	$19.99

FLAMENCO GUITAR
00697363	Method Book/Online Audio	$17.99

FOLK GUITAR
00697414	Method Book/Online Audio	$16.99

JAZZ GUITAR
00695359	Book/Online Audio	$22.99
00697386	Songbook/Online Audio	$16.99

JAZZ-ROCK FUSION
00697387	Book/Online Audio	$24.99

R&B GUITAR
00697356	Book/Online Audio	$19.99
00697433	Songbook/CD Pack	$16.99

ROCK GUITAR
00697319	Book/Online Audio	$19.99
00697383	Songbook/Online Audio	$19.99

ROCKABILLY GUITAR
00697407	Book/Online Audio	$19.99

OTHER METHOD BOOKS

BARITONE GUITAR METHOD
00242055	Book/Online Audio	$12.99

GUITAR FOR KIDS
00865003	Method Book 1/Online Audio	$14.99
00697402	Songbook/Online Audio	$12.99
00128437	Method Book 2/Online Audio	$14.99

MUSIC THEORY FOR GUITARISTS
00695790	Book/Online Audio	$22.99

TENOR GUITAR METHOD
00148330	Book/Online Audio	$14.99

12-STRING GUITAR METHOD
00249528	Book/Online Audio	$22.99

METHOD SUPPLEMENTS

ARPEGGIO FINDER
00697352	6" x 9" Edition	$9.99
00697351	9" x 12" Edition	$10.99

BARRE CHORDS
00697406	Book/Online Audio	$16.99

CHORD, SCALE & ARPEGGIO FINDER
00697410	Book Only	$24.99

GUITAR TECHNIQUES
00697389	Book/Online Audio	$16.99

INCREDIBLE CHORD FINDER
00697200	6" x 9" Edition	$7.99
00697208	9" x 12" Edition	$9.99

INCREDIBLE SCALE FINDER
00695568	6" x 9" Edition	$9.99
00695490	9" x 12" Edition	$9.99

LEAD LICKS
00697345	Book/Online Audio	$12.99

RHYTHM RIFFS
00697346	Book/Online Audio	$14.99

SONGBOOKS

CLASSICAL GUITAR PIECES
00697388	Book/Online Audio	$12.99

EASY POP MELODIES
00697281	Book Only	$7.99
00697440	Book/Online Audio	$16.99

(MORE) EASY POP MELODIES
00697280	Book Only	$7.99
00697269	Book/Online Audio	$16.99

(EVEN MORE) EASY POP MELODIES
00699154	Book Only	$7.99
00697439	Book/Online Audio	$16.99

EASY POP RHYTHMS
00697336	Book Only	$10.99
00697441	Book/Online Audio	$16.99

(MORE) EASY POP RHYTHMS
00697338	Book Only	$9.99
00697322	Book/Online Audio	$16.99

(EVEN MORE) EASY POP RHYTHMS
00697340	Book Only	$7.99
00697323	Book/Online Audio	$16.99

EASY POP CHRISTMAS MELODIES
00697417	Book Only	$9.99
00697416	Book/Online Audio	$16.99

EASY POP CHRISTMAS RHYTHMS
00278177	Book Only	$6.99
00278175	Book/Online Audio	$14.99

EASY SOLO GUITAR PIECES
00110407	Book Only	$12.99

REFERENCE

GUITAR PRACTICE PLANNER
00697401	Book Only	$7.99

GUITAR SETUP & MAINTENANCE
00697427	6" x 9" Edition	$16.99
00697421	9" x 12" Edition	$14.99

For more info, songlists, or to purchase these and more books from your favorite music retailer, go to

halleonard.com

HAL•LEONARD®